Words Are Not for Hurting

You know
lots of words.

Who listens
when you talk?

Your family, your friends, your teachers...

...many people!

How do you use your words?

You say your name
or ask for help.

You tell a story
or sing a song.

Some of your words
are LOUD!

"wheeee!"

And some of your words are soft.

Some of your words are kind.

"I love you."

But some of them are not.

Words are not
for hurting.

What do hurtful words do?

They hurt our ears.
They hurt our feelings.

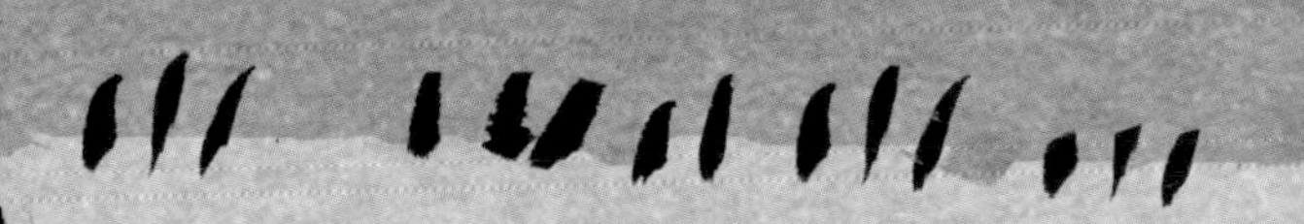

You can do this instead: think before you speak.

And keep hurtful words to yourself.

If the words come out before you can stop them...

"Uh-oh!"

...two other words need to be said:

"I'm sorry."

Those two little words
can be a BIG help.

Words are not for hurting.

Words are for helping!

Tips for Parents and Caregivers

- Use this book interactively. Invite your child to point to the pictures or respond to questions you ask while reading. You might say: 'Why is this girl crying?' or 'How do you think this boy feels?'

- Notice when your child uses words in kind or helpful ways. You could say: 'Thank you for asking for that toy so nicely.'

- Gently intervene when you hear hurtful words. You could take your child aside and say: 'See how sad your friend is because you called him that name? You know how it feels to be sad, too. Let's think of what you can say to help him feel better.' You might add: 'Words are not for hurting.'

- Talk about feelings throughout the day. To learn to use words in helpful ways, children need names for feelings. Help your child notice the feelings of others, too: 'He looks like he feels angry.' or 'I can tell she's unhappy because she's crying.'

- Try the simple reminder: 'Use your words.' Toddlers often scream or cry instead of communicating their needs in words. When your child has something important to express, you might calmly repeat the phrase: 'Use your words.' At first, you may need to do some prompting: 'Are you trying to tell me that you're still hungry?' 'Are you unhappy because you didn't get a turn on the swings?' With repetition, your child will come to know what 'use your words' means, and will begin to have more success with putting thoughts and feelings into words.

- Teach the importance of 'I'm sorry.' Help them to understand that everyone makes mistakes, including adults. Encourage your child to offer an apology when needed. When it's you who slips up, show that you know how to say 'I'm sorry', too. Your child is always learning from your example.

- Be patient. Toddlers naturally think they are the centre of the universe. It can be hard for them to remember to be concerned about how their words and actions affect others. And while language development is different for each child, toddlers are in the process of discovering new ways to express themselves. Often, they don't have the words they need right when they need them. Gradually, they will come to understand that other people have feelings just like they do. Over time, they will have command of more and more words that let them speak in ways that are helpful to them and to others.

First published in the UK in 2009 by A & C Black, an imprint of Bloomsbury Publishing Plc, 50 Bedford Square, London, WC1B 3DP

ISBN 978-1-4081-1507-7 Impression 3 5 7 9 10 8 6 4

A CIP catalogue record for this book is available at the British Library.

Printed in China by Leo Paper Products

This book is produced using paper that is made from wood grown in managed, sustainable forests. It is natural, renewable and recyclable. The logging and manufacturing processes conform to the environmental regulations of the country of origin.